New York Wildlife
Animals & Mammals

Billy Grinslott – Kinsey Marie Books

ISBN - 9781968228514

Chipmunks are found in many areas. Chipmunks are small members of the squirrel family. They like to eat nuts and seeds. Chipmunks are most active during the day, especially at dawn and dusk. They have pouches inside of their cheeks so they can carry food. They are very friendly and will take food from your hand. Chipmunks need about 15 hours of sleep per day. The smallest chipmunk species is Tamias minimus, which is found throughout North America.

There are many squirrels in the wild. You may see a red or gray squirrel. The most popular is the gray squirrel. Squirrels are very acrobatic and can climb trees. Their favorite food is acorns. Squirrels hide their food in many small stashes and can find more than 90% of them later. Squirrels are fast and can run up a tree at 12 miles per hour. Newborn squirrels are blind, deaf, and hairless, and rely on their mother until they mature.

Flying Squirrels don't fly like birds. They don't have wings. They have skin that is attached to their legs. When they jump from a tree, they spread their legs out and glide through the air. Most glides are 30 feet from tree to tree. But they can glide up to 150 feet. They are primarily active at night and are social animals, often living in groups and sharing nests. They have large eyes for night vision, long whiskers for navigating in the dark, and a long, flattened tail for steering during glides.

There are many types of rabbits in the wild. The most common is the cottontail. Rabbits are cute, friendly, and fun to watch. Many people have rabbits for pets. They have soft fluffy fur. They are called cottontails because they have a white fluffy tail that looks like a cotton ball. Rabbits thrive in brushy areas, fields, and wooded habitats.

The hare or jackrabbit is bigger than a cottontail rabbit with longer ears and legs. Their longs legs help them to run fast. They are agile and faster than most rabbits. Jackrabbits or hares have excellent hearing and vision. They have large ears and eyes that are positioned on the sides of their head, giving them a wide field of vision. Hares can change color. They have the ability to change color depending on the season and their surroundings.

Snowshoe hares are famous for their incredible seasonal changing camouflage, turning brown in summer and white in winter to blend in. They are also famous for their huge, fur-lined feet that act like natural snowshoes to help them hop over the snow without sinking in. They can run at speeds up to 30 mph and leap 10-12 feet in a single bound. Not only can they run fast, but they can also swim to evade predators.

Pee-ewe what is that stinky critter with the big bushy tail. It smells bad. Skunks are normally curious and friendly unless you scare them. If you scare them, they will flip their bushy tale at you and spray you with a smelly potion and it stinks. Skunks spray a smelly, sulfur-based liquid from their anal glands as a defense mechanism. The spray can cause eye irritation and temporary blindness. Skunks are highly adaptable and can thrive in many different environments. Skunks have strong forefeet and long claws for digging. Skunks live in dens underground.

Badgers have elongated heads, small ears, and black and white faces. Badgers live underground with other family members. Badgers are very social and live in groups. A badger den or sett can be centuries old and are used by many generations of badgers. Badgers are very territorial, it's best not to bother them is you see one. A group of badgers is called a cete, though they are often called clans. Badgers are largely nocturnal but reduce their activity during periods of cold weather.

Opossums or possums have strong tails and can hang from trees. One trick that a possum has, is when it feels danger is it will play dead. It will lay there and not move. Possums have white to gray face hair. Possums like to eat wood ticks. They are also immune to snakebites. Opossums are susceptible to frostbite because their hands and tails are not protected by fur. Opossums are marsupials, which means they have pouches for their young, like kangaroos and koalas.

Raccoons like to come out at night. Their eyes are made so they can see in the dark. Raccoons are highly intelligent and can solve problems. They can learn to open doors, trash cans, and other containers. They are called masked bandits because they like to raid and eat out of trash cans at night. Raccoons can survive in many environments.

Mallard ducks are by far the most recognizable and popular ducks in the world. They live in just about every area of North America. Their estimated population is around 19 million birds. The male is easily recognizable from its white neck ring and green neck and head. The female Mallard has between five to 14 light green eggs. Most ducks don't have green eggs, so this makes them unique. The male Mallard is called a drake and the female a hen. Female Mallards quack. Males don't quack, instead they produce deeper, raspier one- and two-note calls. They can also make rattling sounds by rubbing their bills against their flight feathers.

Canada Geese are the most sought after and abundant goose in North America. They live in many places. Canada geese can travel 1,500 miles in a day if the weather permits. Canada geese migrate every year. They fly in a V-formation, which allows them to travel long distances without stopping, as they can switch positions and conserve energy. Canada geese are known for their distinctive honk and are sometimes called Canadian honkers.

Grouse, particularly ruffed grouse, are interesting birds known for their unique drumming displays. They flap or rotate their wings, and it sounds like drums beating. During winter, ruffed grouse often burrow into snow. They have comb-like fringes on their toes that act like snowshoes, allowing them to walk easily on snow.

The bobwhite quail has the largest range of any game bird in America. Bobwhite quail are the most common species of quail. The bobwhite is often referred to as the number one game bird of the eastern and southern United States. Bobwhite quail are known for their explosive flight, and social behavior in groups called coveys.

Mourning Doves are unable to sweat. To stay cool during hot weather, they pant just like dog do. Mourning doves eat and collect seeds in their crop, which is an enlarged part of their esophagus. Then they digest them later. It's estimated that there are more than 100 million mourning doves in the US. With the southern states having the biggest population.

Ringed Neck Pheasants are one of the most sought-after birds in North America. They are found throughout most of Northern America and Canada. Ring-necked pheasants are not native to the US. Instead, they were brought here from Asia in the 1880's. While not as widespread as other game birds, they are present in some areas of the state.

Wood ducks are by far one of the coolest looking birds. Males have vibrant colors and long feathers on the back of their head. Wood Ducks are unique among most waterfowl. They need bodies of water that are near trees. They use lakes, ponds, and streams that are adjacent to wooded areas so they can nest in tree cavities.

The Wild Turkey is a large, bird that is native to North America. It is the heaviest bird in the United States and can weigh up to 24 pounds. Only male turkey's gobble. Wild turkeys can fly. Wild turkeys sleep in trees. Their heads can change colors. You can tell a turkey's emotions by the color of their heads. Colors can change from red to blue to white, depending on how excited or calm they are. You can find wild turkeys in just about every state in America.

Beavers use their teeth to cut and knock down trees. They build dams with them to block water, so they have a place to live and swim. They also eat wood. Beavers can stay underwater for about 8 minutes. Beavers slap their tails on the water to indicate danger. Beavers are the largest rodents in North America.

Nutria are large, semi-aquatic rodents known for their orange teeth and webbed hind feet. They are invasive in many areas, where they can cause significant damage. Their burrowing can destroy riverbanks and levees, and their diet of eating vegetation can decimate marshlands. Nutrias are larger than muskrats but smaller than beavers. Their large yellow-orange incisor teeth are used for gnawing and eating plants. Their partially webbed hind feet make them excellent swimmers. Nutrias have relatively poor eyesight and rely more on their hearing to detect danger. Unlike beavers and muskrats, they have a long, round, and mostly hairless tail.

Muskrats are found in marshes, ponds, and streams with abundant aquatic vegetation. Muskrats have a scaly tail that acts as a rudder for swimming and helps them stay afloat. They primarily eat aquatic plants like cattails, sedges, and grasses, but also consume small animals like mussels, crayfish, and fish. They have a second set of lips that close behind their front incisors, enabling them to dive underwater, chew, and eat without swallowing water. They build lodges made of mud and vegetation and also live in burrows along the banks of water sources.

Otters have the thickest fur of any animal. The otter is one of the few mammals that use tools, like rocks to break thing open. A group of otters resting together is called a raft.

Otters primarily rely on their sense of touch, whiskers, and forepaws, in murky waters to locate food. Otters have built in pouches of loose skin under their forearms to stash extra food when diving.

Groundhogs or woodchucks are the largest member of the squirrel family. Groundhogs get their name because of their big bodies, and they live underground. Groundhogs are skilled climbers and swimmers. Groundhogs are true hibernators, sleeping for up to six months. Groundhog Day is where Punxsutawney Phil predicts how long winter will last.

Many Lemmings fur can change color with the seasons. Their front paws have broad, flattened claws for digging. Lemmings live in holes and tunnels that they dig in the ground. In winter they tunnel under the snow. Lemmings eat mosses, roots, and grasses. Lemmings are very small animals, usually, just three to six inches long. Their bodies are covered in thick fur, and they don't hibernate during winter months, they are active year-round.

The American Mink lives across most of North America and is a cat sized. Mink are very skilled climbers and swimmers. They prefer to keep to themselves. They communicate using odors, visual signals, and other sounds. They purr when they're happy, like cats. Mink are agile swimmers, and they often dive to find food

Weasels are the smallest members of the meat-eating animals. Although small, they do not hibernate and are active all winter. Weasels in northern ranges turn white in the winter to camouflage in the snow. Weasels have long whiskers like cats, to help them feel things. They even have long whiskers on their elbows. When a weasel gets annoyed, it stomps its feet, just like humans do. Weasels are quick, agile, and alert animals. They are excellent climbers and swimmers.

The least weasel is the smallest carnivore in North America, weighing only 1 to 2.5 ounces and measuring about 6 to 8 inches long. They can be found in a variety of habitats, including forests, woodlands, grasslands, and brushy fields. Their fur is soft and dense, with brown fur on top and white fur on the underside, including the chin and feet. Weasels are clever and highly intelligent.

The Stoat or ermine is part of the weasel family. Stoats can thrive in many climates and environments. They can live in most habitats if there's food and shelter. Stoats are opportunistic predators that hunt day and night. They have a strong sense of smell and can travel up to 1.5 miles in a few hours. Stoats are good at climbing trees. They can swim and dive underwater. Stoats can reach speeds of up to 20 miles an hour. In colder climates, stoats turn almost completely white, with just a black tip on their tail.

Fishers live in the forests of Canada and the northern United States. They hiss and growl when upset. They are closely related to badgers, mink, and otters. Fisher young are known as kits. Fishers are one of the few animals that eat porcupines. Fishers are also called pekan, pequam, wejack, and woolang.

Martens live in a variety of habitats, including forests, woodlands, and snowy areas. Martens can be distinguished from fishers, because martens are smaller, have orange on their throats and chests, and have pointier ears and snouts. Martens are part of the weasel family. They are very rare and hard to find. Their tail is long, about two thirds of their body size. There are 13 subspecies of American marten that are native to North America.

Porcupines have sharp quills to help protect them. A porcupine can have up to 30 thousand quills. They are sharp and will stick you if you touch them. Porcupines are excellent climbers with long claws. Porcupines are shy, nocturnal, and solitary animals that spend much of their time in trees. To communicate they make grunts and high-pitched noises. A group of porcupines is called a family.

Bobcats are named for their short, bobbed tails with white tips. They have similar markings to lynxes but are much smaller. Bobcats live in a variety of habitats. Bobcats are skilled at leaping and can run up to 30 miles per hour.

Gray fox prefers to live in rocky canyons and ridges but can also be found in wooded areas and open fields. They have strong, hooked claws that enable them to climb trees. Which is abnormal for a dog species. Gray foxes are not observed as frequently as red foxes due to their reclusive nature and more nocturnal habits.

Red foxes have excellent hearing, allowing them to hear rodents digging underground from miles away. When afraid, red foxes grin or look like they are smiling. Red fox's front paws have five toes, while their hind feet only have four. Foxes dig underground dens where they raise their kits and hide from predators. A group of foxes is called a skulk or a leash. Babys are called kits and females are called vixens.

The coyote is bigger than a fox weighing between 20 and 45 pounds. Eastern coyotes are part wolf. Coyotes are great for pest control. They like to eat mice and rats. They can adapt and live almost anywhere, even in the city. Coyotes are very smart and have been observed learning and following traffic signals in some cities. They have a yip type of call when they communicate with each other. Coyotes are found in all the United States, except Hawaii.

The Coywolf got its name because it is a cross between the coyote, wolf and dogs. While coyotes are common, they are smaller than wolves. Coyotes typically weigh around 30-40 pounds, while coywolf hybrids can weigh significantly more, with some reports suggesting specimens of over 60 pounds. They can be significantly larger than a typical coyote.

Yes, there are feral hogs, often called wild boars or hogs, in New York. They are an invasive species found in numerous counties. Feral hogs are also known as wild boars or wild pigs. Feral hogs are known for their high reproductive rates and their tendency to root up the ground, which can lead to habitat destruction. They are highly intelligent, social animals with a keen sense of smell and a surprisingly good memory. Wild pigs can be found in various habitats, including forests, grasslands, and agricultural areas.

Black bears are the smallest members of the bear family in North America. Black Bears love to eat sweet things like berries, fruits, and vegetables. They are good climbers and fast runners. They are excellent swimmers and can paddle at least a mile and a half in freshwater. They usually sleep for long periods of time and hibernate during the winter. They typically try to stay away from people unless they find food in the area.

Yes, there is a small, established population of non-native Sika deer in New York State. They are mostly found on Long Island, with multiple sightings recorded in Southaven County Park. Sika deer are smaller than white-tailed deer and have a more reddish-brown coat with white spots, especially in the summer. Sika deer are known for their various vocalizations, and their excellent swimming abilities. They have at least 10 distinct vocalizations, including soft whistles, loud screams, and horse-like neighs.

The whitetail deer is the most popular deer in North America. Whitetail deer have good eyesight and hearing. They can detect small sounds from a quarter of a mile away. Only male deer grow antlers, which are shed each year. Whitetail deer are good swimmers and will use large streams and lakes to escape predators. A young deer is called a fawn, a male is a buck, and a female is called a doe. They are the most common deer species and live everywhere in North America.

Yes, there are bison in New York, primarily on private ranches and farms raising them as part of conservation efforts. Look for local farms like Skaneateles Buffalo or Mud Creek Bison Ranch. Bison are the largest mammal in North America and weigh up to 2,000 pounds. Bison can run up to 35 miles per hour. They can jump 6 feet vertically and more than 7 feet horizontally. Bison calves are nicknamed red dogs, because of their orange-red color at birth.

There are six different subspecies of moose. Moose are built for cold areas and like living in cold regions with snow. Moose are the largest members of the deer family. Moose are huge and weigh up to 1500 pounds. Moose love water and are good swimmers. Moose have poor eyesight but compensate with a good sense of smell and hearing. At 5 days old they can outrun a person.

Yes, elk have been sighted in New York State, particularly in Sullivan County. They are likely stray individuals from the managed herds in neighboring Pennsylvania Elk are the second largest members of the deer family. Bulls can weigh up to 1,100 lbs. They can run 40 miles per hour and outrun horses. Elk have eyes on the sides of their heads and can see in every direction except directly in front or behind. They make a cool bugling sound when communicating with other elk. It's fun to listen to them.

Fun Facts about New York Animals

1 – New York's official state mammal is the North American Beaver, designated in 1975.

2 – The Opossum is North America's only marsupial. They are the only animals that carry their young in a pouch.

3 - The black bear is the only species of bear in New York. The black bear population is estimated to be around 8 thousand bears.

4 - The largest wild cat in New York is the Bobcat. They typically weigh up to 35 pounds and measure 25 to 30 inches in length.

5 - Coyotes are the most abundant large predator, and they usually prey on small mammals, rats and mice. They can adapt to live anywhere.

6 - Extirpated Species: The bison, gray wolf, and eastern cougar once roamed New York but are no longer present.

7 - The gray fox is the smallest wild canine, member of the dog family.

8 - The state is home to approximately 92 mammal species, 376 bird species, and 71 amphibian/reptile species.

Author Page

Billy Grinslott – Kinsey Marie Books

Copyright, All Rights Reserved

ISBN – 9781968228514

Thanks

www.ingramcontent.com/pod-product-compliance
Lightning Source LLC
Chambersburg PA
CBHW060848270326
41934CB00002B/48